RAPTURE WATCH

By

Chuck Evaline

FOREWORD BY

Dr. Mark T. Barclay

RAPTURE WATCH
ISBN 978-0-9823390-3-9

Copyright © 2012 Chuck Evaline

Chuck Evaline
2108 E. 10th Street
Jeffersonville, IN. 47130
Reslifechurch@sbcglobal.net
www.res-min.org

All Scripture taken from the King James Version Bible.

Published by:

Kingdom
Ministry Publications
877-286-6372
Lansing, Michigan, USA

CONTENTS

ACKNOWLEDGMENTS

I want to thank my Lord, Jesus Christ, for calling me and using me to share His gospel around the world.

Thanks to the people of Resurrection Life Church in Jeffersonville, Indiana for their faithfulness, prayers, and financial support.

A big thanks to my wife, Tami, for being a great partner with me in life and ministry.

Thank you to Jeanine Skaggs for the work she did on this book.

God Bless you All!

— Pastor Chuck

DEDICATION

I dedicate this book to my two daughters and their husbands: Heather and Jeremy Compton, and Lindsey and Tim Best. Also to my nine grandchildren: Trenton, Brennan, Hagan, Landon, Logan, Colson, Graclynn, Irelyn, and Easton.

I love you all. Thanks for being godly people and being a help in the ministry

FOREWORD
By Dr. Mark T. Barclay

This book is a "must read" for every Christian everywhere. I'm personally very alarmed about the day we're living in (and maybe even a little disgusted), trying to fight off the nervousness that many people are ignoring the teachings of Jesus Christ, the Apostle Paul, the Apostle Peter, and John, the revelator, all in the name of modernization.

The Lord is coming – there's no doubt about it. The Bible very specifically declares a second coming, when the Lord will put His foot down upon the earth, begin to put an end to all things, establish His final commissions and assignments, and climax His plan.

However, before that takes place, the Scriptures are clear about one final appearing. We see a portrait of this in many verses. As Dr. Hilton Sutton used to teach, there are many references to the raptures, from Enoch being taken to the eight righteous being delivered from the wrath of God in the flood – and it doesn't seem like they even got wet!

According to Thessalonians, we know that in that last appearing the Lord does not actually come to stand upon the earth to deal with things; but when He comes, we will meet Him in the air, and so we will ever be with Him.

I pray you're not one of the foolish virgins but one of the wise. Remember, Jesus' story of the ten virgins is not about full and empty – it is about wise and foolish. The foolish virgins knew where to get oil all along, yet they ran out by their own negligence.

This book, Rapture Watch, by Pastor Chuck Evaline, is a great instruction manual for those who do not fully understand the Scriptures so they can prepare themselves for the end of all things. It's also a great reminder to all of us who have cherished and held dear these great teachings and doctrines of the kingdom of God. I've always said that endorsing the Scriptures does not make them any more valid or any more true, and not endorsing them does not take anything away from them. They are no less valid, and they are no less true. The Bible is clear on the subject of the catching away of the Church.

No matter what you believe or how you believe it will come to pass, all life is coming to a rapid end, and you don't want to be here if the resistance called "the Church" is removed from the earth. I pray you will study these verses and discern the heart of Pastor Chuck, as he has written a masterpiece to encourage us to look up once again because our redemption draweth nigh. THE LORD IS COMING! And He's coming for a triumphant Church, without spot, wrinkle, blemish, or any such thing. I hope you're included among that group. Enjoy the book, be convicted in your heart, and when you get a moment, congratulate Pastor Chuck for this wonderful helps tool.

INTRODUCTION

Praise the Lord! According to Scripture, we are living in the last days. We very well could be the generation that sees Jesus come and catch His church away.

In no way am I setting dates and times for the Rapture of the Church, because at no place in the Bible are we given a date or a time. But we are given signs to look for that point us to this glorious event. Even though we do not know the exact day of the Rapture, we are to know the season of it.

There are people who like to say, "The Word says Jesus' coming will be like a thief in the night." The

Bible does say that, but let's look at the complete scripture in I Thessalonians 5. In Verse 2, Paul writes:

> 2 *"For yourselves know perfectly that the day of the Lord so cometh a s a thief in the night."*

If we read on, in Verses 4 and 5, we see these words:

> 4 *"But ye, brethren, are not in darkness, that that day should overtake you as a thief."*

> 5 *"Ye are all the children of light and the children of the day. We are not of the night, or of the darkness."*

As born-again, Spirit-filled believers who know the Word of God, we are not in the dark, but by the light of God's Word (see Psalm 119:105), we see what is ahead. And although we may not know the day or the time, we know we are getting close.

This book is intended to be an easy-to-understand guide through the Scriptures, but not so theologically deep that the average believer cannot understand it.

I pray that by the time you finish this book, you, too, will be on alert and be on a RAPTURE WATCH.

CHAPTER 1

What is the Rapture?

WHAT IS THE RAPTURE OF THE CHURCH?

Although the word "Rapture" is not found in English Bibles, the word "Rapture" means to be caught up or snatched away. The Rapture of the Church means the Church will be caught up or snatched away by the Lord.

In the study of end-time events, there are three events to consider: the Rapture of the Church, the seven-year Tribulation Period, and the Millennial Reign of Jesus

Christ on the earth after the Tribulation. The Bible, I believe, teaches that the Rapture of the Church will happen just before the seven-year Tribulation begins (more on this later).

Look at 1 Thessalonians 4:13-18:

13 "But I would not have you to be ignorant, brethren, concerning them which are asleep, that ye sorrow not, even as others which have no hope."

14 "For if we believe that Jesus died and rose again, even so them also which sleep in Jesus will God bring with Him."

15 "For this we say unto you by the Word of the Lord, that we which are alive and remain unto the coming of the Lord shall not prevent them which are asleep."

16 "For the Lord Himself shall descend from Heaven with a shout, with the voice of the archangel, and with the trump of God: and the dead in Christ shall rise first."

17 "Then we which are alive and remain shall be caught up together with them in the clouds, to meet the Lord in the air: and so shall we ever be with the Lord."

18 "Wherefore comfort one another with these words."

The Rapture is not to be confused with the Second Coming of Jesus. During the Rapture, Jesus will not set foot on the earth, but will come in the clouds (see 1 Thessalonians 4:16-17). When this event occurs, the Lord (Jesus) will descend from Heaven with a shout, and the trump of God will sound, and the Church will be Raptured, or caught up into the clouds to be with the Lord forever.

Why do I believe the Rapture will happen before the Tribulation Period begins? The Bible gives us examples to look at and compare. The Tribulation Period will be a terrible time on the earth, as judgment is poured out.

Look at Genesis 7. Noah had followed God's instructions to build the ark so that he and his family and the animals could be saved from the coming flood and destruction. In Chapter 7, it says:

1 "And the Lord said to Noah, Come thou and all thy house into the ark; for thee have I seen righteous before me in this generation."

16 "And they that went in ... as God commanded him; and the Lord shut him in."

The Bible then says the flood came on the earth. Just before the destruction, God removed the righteous people so they would not be destroyed.

As a side note, 2 Peter 2:5 says that Noah was a preacher of righteousness. This verse tells us that God had a man preaching the Word of God, so that more people could escape the destruction. Obviously, the people rejected his message. The Lord was not trying to keep people out; the people simply did not listen. Today, the Lord does not want anyone to miss the Rapture, but many will refuse to hear the Gospel.

Noah entering the ark and missing the flood was God's provision to escape the destruction, an example of the Rapture.

Another example is in Genesis 19. Here, Lot and his family are living in Sodom, a very wicked place. The Lord is going to judge this wicked place and destroy it. Before He destroys it, He sends angels to get Lot and his family out (see Verse 1).

In Verse 15, we read:

15 "And when the morning arose, then the angels hastened Lot, saying, Arise, take thy wife, and thy two daughters, which are here; lest thou be consumed in the iniquity of the city."

Lot, his wife, and two daughters got out of Sodom, and Verse 24 says that God rained upon Sodom and upon Gomorrah brimstone and fire from the Lord out of Heaven. In other words, destruction came, and God got the righteous out before the judgment. This is another example of the Rapture.

When Jesus gave John the Revelation, He gave us something to let us know the Rapture would occur prior to the Tribulation. In Revelation Chapters 2 and 3, the Lord is talking to the churches in Asia. In these two chapters, the word "church" is used many times.

Chapter 4 Verse 1 says: "After this …" After what? After dealing with the Church, a door opened in Heaven, and John heard a voice that was like a trumpet which said, "Come up hither …" Remember what we read in 1 Thessalonians 4: when the Rapture happens, there will be a shout and a trumpet (Verse 16).

Interestingly, after the words "Come up hither" are spoken, the word "church" is never used in the rest of the Book of Revelation, especially during the Tribulation Period. Why is this? Because the Church has been raptured and is gone.

One last thought on this topic. 2 Thessalonians 2:8 says that the wicked one will be revealed. The Amplified Bible says, "… The lawless and the antichrist will be revealed …" The antichrist comes to power during the Tribulation.

When will the antichrist be revealed? 2 Thessalonians 2:7 (amp) says, "… When he who restrains is taken out of the way." When the Church is taken out of the way, when the Rapture takes place, the antichrist will be revealed and the Tribulation will be underway.

The Rapture is going to happen. 1 Corinthians 15:52 says it will happen in a moment, in the twinkling of an eye. By the time you finish this book, I believe you will agree that it could happen very soon.

For the believer in Jesus, and those living for Him, the Rapture is not to be feared, but is something to look forward to. 1 Thessalonians 4:18 tells us to comfort one another with words about the Rapture. I encourage and comfort you with these words.

For two thousand years, Christians have waited for the Rapture of the Church. We could be the generation to experience it. The world is bad and getting worse. It is not a bad thing to be taken out of here by the Lord Himself.

If you are as old as me, you may remember a commercial that portrayed a woman in a bathtub after a hard day. The woman would mention the product's name and then say, "Take me away ..."

This earth is a hard, evil place. Say this: "Jesus, take me away." One day, through the Rapture, He will.

CHAPTER 2

What is a Rapture Watch?

Imagine you are watching television or listening to the radio, and all of a sudden you hear the following: "BEEP! BEEP! BEEP! The National Weather Service has issued a tornado watch for your area. A watch does not mean that a tornado is occurring at this time, but a watch means that conditions are favorable for a tornado to occur at any moment. Please stay alert. We now return you to your regular programming."

Hopefully, if you hear something like this, you will

begin to think about what you need to do to be safe if a tornado comes. You may not yet go to a basement or other safe place, but you will get ready, at least in your mind.

Weather watches are not issued to scare people. Meteorologists and newscasters do not break into programs with watches in order to cause fear. No: they break into the programs to prepare you for what may be coming your way.

The people who make these decisions do so after studying charts, graphs, and computer information. They are looking for certain signs. When they see these signs, they know a tornado could happen, and they begin to tell people to get ready.

Weather forecasters have a responsibility to let people know what is coming. Preachers of the Gospel must feel the same responsibility.

The Bible is clear on what will be happening on the earth before the Rapture of the Church. I believe that on earth today, we are under a Rapture Watch.

Conditions are favorable for the Rapture of the Church to happen at any moment.

What are the signs? Read on.

CHAPTER 3

Who is going in the Rapture?

Look again at 1 Thessalonians 4. In this Chapter, the Apostle Paul gives information concerning the Rapture of the Church. In Verse 13, Paul writes:

> 13 *"But I would not have you to be ignorant, brethren ..."*

By using the word "brethren," Paul is referring to fellow Christians – people who have been born again.

If these were the only Scriptures concerning the Rapture of the Church, one could conclude that all born-again people will go in the Rapture.

Let's consider some other Scriptures. Look at Matthew, Chapter 25. Here, Jesus gives us the parable of the ten virgins:

1 "Then shall the kingdom of heaven be likened unto ten virgins, which took their lamps, and went forth to meet the bridegroom."

2 "And five of them were wise, and five were foolish."

3 "They that were foolish took their lamps and took no oil with them."

4 "But the wise took oil in their vessels with their lamps."

5 "While the bridegroom tarried, they all slumbered and slept."

6 "And at midnight, there was a cry made, Behold, the bridegroom cometh; go ye out to meet him."

7 "Then all those virgins arose, and trimmed their lamps."

8 "And the foolish said unto the wise, give us of your oil; for our lamps are gone out."

9 "But the wise answered, saying, not so; lest there be

not enough for us and you: but go ye rather to them that sell, and buy for yourselves."

10 "And while they went to buy, the bridegroom came; and they that were ready went in with him to the marriage: and the door was shut."

11 "Afterward came also the other virgins, saying, Lord, Lord, open to us."

12 "But he answered and said, Verily I say unto you, I know you not."

13 "Watch therefore, for ye know neither the day nor the hour wherein the Son of man cometh."

You may ask, "What does this have to do with who is going in the Rapture?" In Verse 10, Jesus says the bridegroom came and they went with him to the marriage. I believe this refers to the Rapture of the Church.

Again, the question is: Who is going in the Rapture?

We are told there are ten virgins. A virgin is someone pure, and represents people who have been born again.

2 Corinthians 5:17 says:

> *17 "Therefore if any man be in Christ, he is a new creature: old things are passed away; behold all things are become new."*

The old nature – the sin nature – is gone, and you are new and pure.

In 2 Peter 3:1, the Apostle Peter tells the believers to stir up their pure minds.

1 John 1:7 says:

> *7 "… the blood of Jesus Christ his Son cleanseth us from all sin."*

If a person makes Jesus Christ the Lord of their life, His blood cleanses that person from all sin, or makes them pure (I John 1:9). As I maintained earlier, the ten virgins represent ten born-again people.

Jesus went on to say that five of these virgins were wise and five were foolish. What does it mean to be wise or foolish? In Matthew 7, Jesus told us the difference between someone who acts wisely and someone who acts foolishly. Start reading in Verse 24:

24 "Therefore whosoever heareth these sayings of mine, and doeth them, I will liken him unto a wise man ..."

So a wise man is one who hears the Word of God and does it.

We are told in Verse 26:

26 "And everyone that heareth these sayings of mine, and doeth them not, shall be likened unto a foolish man ..."

A foolish man is one who hears the Word of God, but doesn't do it. James said that anyone who hears the Word of God but does not do it is deceiving themselves (James 1:22). I believe that a person is foolish if they deceive themselves.

Even though all "ten virgins" were born again, five were hearing and doing the Word of God; and five were hearing it, but not doing it. No doubt, all of the virgins had been told that the bridegroom could come to get them at any moment. It appears that five believed, and five did not. The five who believed it lived by the Word of God and stayed full of oil; the other five born-again people did not believe He was coming and did not live by the Word of God, and their oil level was low. Five were ready to go and five were not.

"But Preacher, it says they all slept. Shouldn't they have stayed awake?" I had the Lord minister to me that it was all right for the five wise virgins to sleep – they were ready to go – but the foolish should have stayed awake and gotten ready. It's as if two people are having a test tomorrow. The one who is ready can go to sleep at night, but the one who is not ready had better stay up and get ready!

Verse 6 says the cry was made at midnight; that the bridegroom was coming and the virgins should meet him. The parable goes on to say in Verse 7 that they all turned up their lamps to go meet the bridegroom, but the foolish virgins' light was not very bright because they were low on oil. Because of this, their light was going out. The foolish virgins asked the wise virgins to share their oil, and the wise virgins said no.

The lesson here is that a person cannot live on the faith of other people. You and I will not go in the Rapture holding onto someone else's "coattails." We all must be full of oil.

The next point is very sad to me. Verse 9 says that the wise virgins told the foolish virgins to go buy their own oil. In Verse 10, it says, "… they went to buy …" Notice that they did not say, "But we don't know where to go." No! They knew where to go but had chosen not to go, and because of that, their oil level was too low.

This is what we see today. There are born-again people who refuse to go to hear the Word preached. They know where it is being preached, but they choose to go to the "feel good" church, or to the "play" church, or not to go at all. Because of this, the oil they once had has leaked out.

Hebrews 2:1 says:

> *1 "Therefore we ought to give the more earnest heed to the things which we have heard, lest at any time we should let them slip."*

In the margin of my Bible it says that the phrase "let them slip" can be translated, "Run out as leaking vessels."

If we do not stay full of the Word, full of oil, and full of light by constantly and consistently hearing and doing the Word of God, then the Word we once had will leak out. Even though we are born again, we may be left behind when the Rapture happens.

Finally, Hebrews 9:28 says:

> *28 "... and unto them that look for him (Jesus) shall he appear the second time without sin to salvation."*

Many people, even born-again people, are not looking for Jesus to come because they do not believe He is coming. Why? Because they have never heard the Word preached about the Rapture of the Church.

The Lord will never force any of His blessings on anyone. If a person is born again they will go to Heaven, but that does not mean they will experience the Rapture. Matthew 25:10 says that the ones that were ready went in with the bridegroom. It is one thing to get ready; it is quite another thing to stay ready.

Do not allow the oil to leak out, so that when the question is asked, "Who is going in the Rapture?" you can say, "I am!"

CHAPTER 4
Glory and Darkness

The world we live in is a very dark place. I recently turned 50 years old, and the world I live in does not resemble the world I was raised in.

I remember a world where Christians were treated with respect, even by those who did not claim to be Christians. The world's people may have had filthy mouths, but if a preacher or another believer was around, they would clean up their language and apologize if a bad word slipped out.

Nowadays, there is little to no honor or respect for anyone claiming to be a believer in Jesus. This is a sign of the darkness that is covering the earth.

Isaiah 60:1-2 says:

> 1 *"Arise, shine; for thy light is come, and the glory of the LORD is risen upon thee."*
>
> 2 *"For, behold, the darkness shall cover the earth, and gross darkness the people: but the LORD shall arise upon thee, and his glory shall be seen upon thee."*

Isaiah was seeing, by God's Spirit, the day we are living in – darkness covering the earth and the gross darkness of the people. In the Amplified Bible, gross darkness is called "dense darkness," or, we could say, thick darkness. The people of the world are being covered by thick darkness, and many are being destroyed.

My Pastor, Dr. Mark T. Barclay, had a vision many years ago wherein he saw this gross darkness coming on the earth. In this darkness was every form of evil and vile thing imaginable. This is what is here now, and it is only going to get worse before the Rapture of the

Church. Paul said in 2 Timothy 3:13 that in the last days, evil men would grow worse and worse.

Isaiah also saw God's glory coming on God's people at the same time the darkness was coming on the earth. Let's examine this idea of God's glory. Look at Ezekiel 1:26-28.

> *26 "And above the firmament that was over their heads was a likeness of a throne, as the appearance of a sapphire stone: and upon the likeness of the throne was the likeness as the appearance of a man above upon it."*

> *27 "And I saw as the colour of amber, as the appearance of fire round about within it, from the appearance of his loins even upward, and from the appearance of his loins even downward, I saw as it were the appearance of fire, and it had brightness round about."*

> *28 "… This was the appearance of the likeness of the glory of the Lord."*

Here we see the prophet Ezekiel describing God's glory as fire. In Ezekiel's day, fire was the only source of light the people had. When Isaiah said that God's glory would be seen on His people, we could say, I believe, that God's light would be seen on His people: not necessarily a natural light, but the light of God's love and power.

JESUS – THE LIGHT OF THE WORLD

We read in John 8:12:

> 12 *"Then spake Jesus again unto them, saying, I am the light of the world: he that followeth me shall not walk in darkness, but shall have the light of life."*

Jesus said that He is the light of the world, and those that follow Him shall not be in darkness.

In John Chapter 1 Verse 1, it says:

> 1 *"In the beginning was the Word, and the Word was with God, and the Word was God."*
>
> 4 *"In Him ... (the Word) ... was life; and the life was the light of men."*
>
> 5 *"And the light shineth in darkness; and the darkness comprehended it not."*

In the Amplified Bible, Verse 5 says that the darkness has never overpowered the light, or put it out. So

Jesus is the light of the world. Jesus is the Word of God, and in the Word is the light that darkness cannot overpower.

Psalm 119:130 says, "The entrance of thy words giveth light, ..." When we have the Word of God in us, we have God's light in and on us.

PEOPLE – THE LIGHT OF THE WORLD

Jesus said that He is the light of the world. In Matthew 5:14, He said that believers in Him – those who are born again and connected to Him – are the light of the world. We who are believers in Jesus are the light of the world because Jesus lives in us.

I like to say it this way: Jesus is the match and we are the candle. A candle cannot produce its own light, but can only be a carrier of light from another source. Jesus is our source of light. In verse 15-16, Jesus called us a candle.

When a person is born again, the Holy Spirit causes the human spirit to come alive. Jesus said that born-

again people should be filled, or baptized, in the Holy
Ghost. See Acts 1:4-8:

> 4 *"And, being assembled together with them, com-
> manded them that they should not depart from
> Jerusalem, but wait for the promise of the Father,
> which, saith he, ye have heard of me."*

> 5 *"For John truly baptized with water; but ye shall
> be baptized with the Holy Ghost not many days
> hence."*

> 6 *"When they therefore were come together, they
> asked of him, saying, Lord, wilt thou at this time re-
> store again the kingdom to Israel?"*

> 7 *"And he said unto them, It is not for you to know
> the times or the seasons, which the Father hath put in
> his own power."*

> 8 *"But ye shall receive power, after that the Holy
> Ghost is come upon you: and ye shall be witnesses
> unto me both in Jerusalem, and in all Judaea, and in
> Samaria, and unto the uttermost part of the earth."*

In Matthew 3:11, John the Baptist referring to Jesus,
said:

> 11 *"... he shall baptize you with the Holy Ghost, and*

with fire."

In Acts 2, the Bible tells us that believers were gathered for the Holy Spirit, as Jesus instructed them in Acts 1:4.

Acts 2:1-4a says:

1 "And when the day of Pentecost was fully come, they were all with one accord in one place."

2 "And suddenly there came a sound from heaven as a rushing mighty wind, and it filled all the house where they were sitting."

3 "And there appeared unto them cloven tongues like as of fire and it sat upon each of them."

4 "And they were all filled with the Holy Ghost ..."

The Apostle Peter said in Acts 5:3-4 that the Holy Ghost is God. When a person is filled with the Holy Ghost, that person has God living inside him. By the Holy Ghost, the light of God is in and on a person's life.

We have seen here that God's glory – God's light – is going to be seen on people that are born again and baptized in the Holy Ghost, and who continue to fill themselves with the Word of God. When a person is full of God's light, the darkness cannot win.

Believers are to be a light in this dark world. There should be no question whether someone is in darkness or light – the difference should be clearly seen.

DIVISION BETWEEN LIGHT AND DARKNESS

Remember what Isaiah said in Chapter 60 Verse 2. He said gross darkness would cover the people, but God's glory would be seen on you.

At the time darkness is covering some people, God's glory, or light, would be seen on His people. In other words, there would be a division or difference between those in the light and those in darkness.

In the book of Exodus, God is using Moses to get Israel out of Egypt and the plagues are coming on Egypt. God says in Exodus 8:23:

> 23 "I will put a division between my people and thy people ..."

The Lord says here that the trouble coming on Egypt (representing the world) will not touch God's people.

In Chapter 10 of Exodus, one of the plagues was thick darkness in Egypt (Exodus 10:22). The Word of God tells us in Exodus 10:23 that it was dark in Egypt, but where God's people lived, it was light. The people of the world were in thick, gross darkness, but God's people were in the light.

Remember, the Lord said in Exodus 8:23 that He would put a division between the world's people and His people. In the reference margin of my Bible, it indicates that the word "division" can be translated as "redemption."

The Bible tells us in 1 Peter 1:18-19 that a person is redeemed by the precious blood of Jesus. When a person receives Jesus as Lord of their life, they are redeemed. In other words, that person is called out of darkness into God's marvelous light (1 Peter 2:9).

The Apostle Paul said in 1 Thessalonians 5:5 that born-again believers are children of light and not of darkness. Just as in the days of Moses in Egypt, before God took them out of Egypt and led them to the Promised Land, the world was in darkness, but God's people were in light. This is the type of world we are in today.

In these last days before the Rapture of the Church, everyone needs to understand that the world is dark and getting darker, but the people of God are supposed to have the glory of God shining on our lives. The people of God have been redeemed out of darkness.

After God brought Israel out of Egypt, out of bondage, out of darkness, the only thing a lot of them could talk about was going back. As born-again believers, we never want to go back. There is nothing back there for us but darkness.

Let me close this chapter with an experience I once had while ministering in Jamaica. We were going home from a meeting with a big, full moon in front of us. As I talked with the Pastor I looked back and the moon was gone. After a few minutes I began to see the rim of the moon; there had been a full lunar eclipse. You may ask, what does that have to do with the light of God? I learned in science class that the moon does not produce light, it only reflects the light of the sun. In Genesis 1 on the fourth day of creation it says God made two great lights, the greater one (the sun) to rule the day, and the lesser one (the moon) to rule the night. (See Genesis 1:16-18.)

In John 9:4, Jesus said that while He was in the earth it was day. Jesus is the light of the day (the sun). When Jesus left the earth it became "night" or "dark" in the earth and He left us, the Church, his disciples (the moon). As we are in this world we are to reflect the light of Jesus. Now, back to that lunar eclipse in Jamaica. The Lord asked me, "What caused that eclipse?" I said the earth got between the sun and the moon and the moon's light was put out. The Lord said, "That is correct" and then He said, "You as the light of the world cannot shine if you allow the earth, the world, to get between you and Jesus."

We are in the light. Let's walk in the light, as God is in the light (1 John 1:7). The only way we can do that in these dark last days is to stay connected to Jesus and allow His light to shine through and on us.

CHAPTER 5
Signs in the Earth

In this chapter, I do not want to overload you with statistics, but I will share a few.

Jesus told us that before He comes, there would be political and physical signs in the earth. Look at Matthew 24. In Verse 6, Jesus said there would be "wars and rumors of wars."

The United States alone is dealing with wars in Iraq and Afghanistan, and there are rumors of wars with North Korea, Iran, and many Arab nations. Much blood has been shed and is being shed on the continent of Africa, in tribal wars and in civil wars. There are conflicts between Israel and its Arab neighbors. It seems that in every corner of the globe, there are wars and rumors of wars.

In Matthew 24:7, Jesus gives us more signs in the earth to look for. One sign is famine. I am 50 years old, and I can remember as a little boy seeing pictures on television of starving children in other countries, with their bloated bellies. We hear about places where people are not only starving for food, but also for clean drinking water. In some cases, the famine is a lack of medicine and other medical supplies. Whatever it may be, many people in the world are going without physical needs being met. They are in a famine situation. Man-made programs and ideas help these people to a certain extent, but only the power of Jesus Christ can truly feed all the people.

Also in Verse 7, Jesus talks about pestilences. In Strong's Concordance Greek dictionary, "pestilence" is word number 3,061. It can be translated as "pest" – an insect or other pest – but it can also be translated as "plague" or "disease." Today, we have some of the greatest doctors and medical knowledge ever, but still there are illnesses for which medical science has little or no answers. AIDS and cancer are two of the biggest diseases for which there are no known cures. In the recent past, the world has tried to deal with the H1N1 flu and the West Nile virus, just to name a couple. We are definitely seeing more pestilence.

In Verse 7, Jesus said that a sign of His coming would be earthquakes in divers, or various, places. Unless you have been on another planet, you know we have had an increase in earthquake activity. In 2010, I kept a running list of major earthquakes and what they registered on the Richter scale. Here is a partial list:

January	Haiti	7.9
February	Chile	8.8
February	Turkey	6.0
April	Indonesia	7.9
April	China	6.9

In October, there was an earthquake in the state of Oklahoma, which is known for tornadoes, but not earthquakes.

Besides earthquakes in 2010, there were other natural disasters. In April, there was a major volcano eruption in Iceland, which affected air travel and caused other problems. Also in April, there was a massive mud slide in Brazil.

If the only sign Jesus had given us for His coming had been earthquakes, we would have enough information to issue a Rapture Watch.

Luke 21 gives the same signs to warn us. In Verse 36, Jesus said:

> 36 *"Watch ye therefore, and pray always, that you may be accounted worthy to escape all these things that shall come to pass and to stand before the Son of Man."*

We know from Scripture that when God says something will come to pass, we can count on it. We are witnessing these signs come to pass now, in this day we live in. These signs are another Biblical reason we are under a Rapture Watch.

CHAPTER 6
Deception

Let's turn our attention to probably the most dangerous force the Body of Christ will face in these last days – the force of deception.

In Matthew 24 Verse 3, Jesus is asked: "What will be the sign of your coming?" We read Jesus' answer starting in Verse 4:

> 4 "And Jesus answered and said unto them, Take heed that no man deceive you."

> 5 "For many will come in my name, saying, I am Christ; and shall deceive many."

> 6 "And you shall hear of wars and rumors of war: see that ye be not troubled: for all these things must come to pass, but the end is not yet."

7 *"For nation shall rise against nation, and kingdom against kingdom: and there shall be famines, and pestilences, and earthquakes, in divers' places."*

8 *"All these are the beginnings of sorrows."*

9 *"Then shall they deliver you up to be afflicted, and shall kill you: and ye shall be hated of all nations for my name's sake."*

10 *"And then shall many be offended, and shall betray one another, and shall hate one another."*

11 *"And many false prophets shall rise, and shall deceive many."*

Notice in this list of signs Jesus told us to look for, wars are mentioned one time, famines are mentioned one time, and earthquakes are mentioned one time, but Jesus mentions deception three times. Jesus brings it up again in Verse 24:

24 *"For there shall arise false Christs, and false prophets, and shall show great signs and wonders; insomuch that, if it were possible, they shall deceive the very elect."*

People will ask: If he can do signs and wonders, how is that deceptive? Because the Bible says in 2 Thessalonians 2:9 that there are lying wonders. In other words, what some people do appear to be great signs and wonders, but are nothing more than magic tricks and sleight of hand. What people need to look at is not what great miracles are taking place, but rather the lifestyle and character of the people working these so-called "miracles."

This was seen all the way back in Moses' day. Moses was sent by God to get Israel free from Egypt. In Exodus 4:17, God ordains Moses to use the rod in his hand to do signs. When Moses went into Pharaoh and threw the rod on the ground, it became a serpent (Exodus 7:10). Verses 11–12 say that Pharaoh's magicians did their enchantments, and their rods became serpents.

We see that what Moses did was ordained by God – it was a sign and a wonder – but what the magicians did was a lying wonder. God was not in it.

1 Kings 19 tells of an encounter Elijah had with the Lord. Elijah was hiding from Jezebel. He was in a cave,

and the Lord came to talk with him. In Verse 11, the Lord told Elijah to go stand on the mountain before him. The Bible says that the Lord passed by, and then three things happened:

1) A great and strong wind tore the mountains.

2) An earthquake.

3) A fire.

These are three events that appear powerful to our human senses, but the Word says that God was not in any of them. Then the Lord spoke in a still, small voice.

Just because the event is bright and loud and flashy does not mean that God is in the house. The Lord can show Himself loud and powerful, but just because it appears to be loud and powerful does not mean God is in it.

Paul tells us in 2 Timothy 3:8 that the magicians' names were Jannes and Jambres. The purpose of their lying wonders was to withstand or resist Moses, just as those who today preach false doctrines and work lying wonders are resisting the truth of God's Word, and the truth of God's miracle-working power, and are deceiving people in great numbers.

Look at 2 Thessalonians 2:1-3:

1 "Now we beseech you, brethren, by the coming of our Lord Jesus Christ, and by our gathering together unto him ..."

This Verse refers to the Rapture of the Church.

2 "That you be not soon shaken in mind, or be troubled, neither by spirit, nor by word, nor by letters as from us, as that the day of Christ is at hand."

3 "Let no man deceive you by any means: for that day shall not come, except there come a falling away first, and that man of sin be revealed, the son of perdition."

Verse 3 lets us know we cannot be deceived unless we allow ourselves to be deceived. The purpose for the deception is to get people to fall away from the Word of God, the Church, and ultimately the Lord Himself.

1 Timothy 4:1 says:

1 "Now the Spirit speaketh expressly, that in the latter times some shall depart from the faith, giving heed to seducing spirits, and doctrines of devils."

A seducing spirit causes deception. People are deceived by seducing spirits.

Let's look at an example of how this works. If a person was involved in adultery, and they had been taught that adultery was a sin and that they should not do it, they would feel guilty. One night, they turned on the television and there was a person who claimed to be a preacher, and he said that adultery was not wrong, that it was old-fashioned to think that way. If that person in adultery followed that person, they were deceived by a seducing spirit; they turn from the truth and are on their way to hell unless they repent.

2 Timothy 4:3 says:

3 "For the time will come when they will not endure sound doctrine; but after their own lusts shall heap to themselves teachers, having itching ears."

In other words, people will only listen to "preachers" that make them feel good and comfortable in their sin. This is deception.

4 "And they shall turn away their ears from the truth, and shall be turned unto fables."

Let me give you an example of someone who only wants to feel good and not be convicted. I will call him Sam. I had known Sam for a few years. He was always happy and telling jokes. On Sunday mornings Sam loved to drive past our church on his way to his church. Each week, as we were preparing for church, he would pass and honk his horn to say hi. One day I saw Sam in a store and we had a chuckle over his weekly horn blowing. I said, "Sam, I know you have a home church but some Sunday stop in and be with us." Sam got very serious and said, "No, I can't do that." I said, "why not?" This was Sam's response: "I can sin and go to my church and not feel bad about my sin, but I will be convicted if I come to your church." Sam was more concerned with feeling good than hearing the word, repenting, and being right with God.

Anyone who turns from the truth to a fable is deceived.

These are all signs of deception, and a sign of the soon-coming Rapture of the Church. This is another reason we are under a Rapture Watch. People are turning from the truth to fables. People are falling away. Jesus told us in Matthew 24 not to allow ourselves to be deceived.

Let's close this chapter by looking at John Chapter 8. In Verses 31-32, Jesus said:

> 31 *"If ye continue in my word, then are ye my disciples indeed;"*

> 32 *"And ye shall know the truth, and the truth shall make you free."*

Notice that Jesus said to continue in His Word, not turn from it. When you know the truth, you cannot be deceived.

You probably know that 2 + 2 = 4. If someone told you that 2 + 2 = 5, or 2 + 2 = 3, or 2 + 2 = 100, you would not believe them because you know the truth.

The same is true of the Word of God: study and hear it preached in faith so that you know it. Then when someone tries to deceive you, you will not be moved.

Because of all the lies and deception going on in the world today, we are under a Rapture Watch.

CHAPTER 7
Human Behavior

Let's begin this chapter by reading from II Timothy 3.

1 "This know also, that in the last days perilous times shall come."

I think we have to say we are living in the last days, and we are living in perilous times. When you look at the way prices are going through the proverbial roof, when you see the natural disasters and how much evil is in the world, it is easy to see that we no longer live in the world of "I Love Lucy," "Ozzie and Harriet," or "Mayberry."

2 "For men shall be lovers of their own selves, covetous, boasters, proud, blasphemers, disobedient to parents, unthankful, and unholy."

Today it seems that most people are not concerned with other people, as long as they get what is "theirs." Even people blessed by the Lord are not thankful. They just ask the question, "Is that all?" In other words, they are not thankful but always wanting more.

3 "Without natural affection, trucebreakers, false accusers, incontinent, fierce, despisers of those that are good."

Where to start? When a woman will abort her unborn baby or throw her child from a moving car, that is without natural affection. When a man will turn his back on his children and not support them, that is without natural affection. All these things are happening in our world today.

As far as trucebreakers and false accusers, there are more legal actions and court cases today than ever in the history of the world.

According to Strong's Concordance, the word Incontinent means to have no self control. All we have to do is look at overweight Americans, and we see a self control issue. As for people being fierce: recently in a neighboring state, a woman killed a pregnant woman by cutting her throat, and then cut the baby from the dead woman's body. This is fierce.

People will despise those who are good. You often hear people putting down Christians and talking good about adulterers, robbers, liars, and cheats. All signs of the last days.

4 "Traitors, heady, highminded, lovers of pleasures more than lovers of God."

As I comment on these verses I am giving you my observations from over thirty years of ministry. From the late 1970s until now, I have seen these problems come more and more to the forefront of society, and even in the church.

Today, people are traitors. Again, according to Strong's Concordance, traitor can also mean betrayer.

There are many people – including preachers – who have been or are being betrayed in these last days.

People are heady and highminded. They depend upon and have more faith in their secular education than they do in the Word of God. It is difficult for these people to walk in faith, because most of the time faith makes no sense to a person's mind.

During the last days, people love pleasure more than they love God. I can remember when I played little league baseball in the 1960s and 1970s. At that time it was against the rules to even practice on Sunday. Now, they play games on Sundays, and many Christians will miss church in order to attend these games.

For most people, it seems that the attitude toward God and the things of God is, "If we can fit it in we will, but we are busy." Yeah, busy doing what brings their flesh pleasure instead of pleasing the Lord.

Some of the excuses people give God and their Pastor for not being in Church would never work with their boss. Most people would not miss work to go to their child's game, program, or recital, but they will miss church for those things. Most people would not take time off from work to go fishing, golfing, or bowling, or to work in the yard or clean the house; but they will take time off from church to do these things.

Most parents would not take their children out of school events to go to church, but they will take them out of church for activities. What are children taught? Parents tell them it is important to go to church, read the Bible and pray, yet their activities and pleasures seem to take precedence over the things of God. For the most part, people believe God is good and that serving God is good, as long as it doesn't interfere with "my life." How many times have I heard, "Pastor, I can't do that, I have a life."

Everyone needs to realize we have no life without Jesus. We all need to love the Lord more than the pleasures of this world.

5 *"Having a form of godliness, but denying the power thereof."*

Again, many people attend church fairly regularly, yet continue to live like the world. II Corinthians 6:17 tells us to come out from among the ways of the world and the unclean things.

Today, a common message being taught is that we are saved by grace, so that we may do whatever, because grace covers it. This is not biblical; it is religious, but not biblical. The book of Titus says in Chapter 2: 11-12:

> *11 "For the grace of God that bringeth salvation hath appeared to all men."*

> *12 "Teaching us that, denying ungodliness and worldly lusts, we should live soberly, righteously, and godly, in this present world."*

Yes, we are saved by grace, and that grace tells us to live clean in this dirty world.

Many people are just playing church. They want to act like "Holy Joe" on Sunday morning and "unholy terror" the rest of the week.

Paul said in Romans 1:16 that the Gospel of Christ is the power of God unto salvation. People are turning away from the Gospel of Christ, the Word of God. In verse 13 of II Timothy 3, Paul says that in the last days evil men and seducers shall wax (grow) worse and worse, deceiving and being deceived.

Today, when a person thinks they have heard the worst news ever, it seems that the next day you hear something even worse. People are being deceived and are turning from the word of God, and from the faith (I Timothy 4:1), and are turning to fables (II Timothy 4:3-4). These are definitely signs that activate a Rapture Watch.

I Timothy 4:1:

> *1 "Now the Spirit speaketh expressly, that in the latter times some shall depart from the faith, giving heed to seducing spirits, and doctrines of devils ..."*

II Timothy 4:3-4:

> *3 "For the time will come when they will not endure sound doctrine; but after their own lusts shall they heap to themselves teachers, having itching ears;"*

> *4 "And they shall turn away their ears from the truth, and shall be turned unto fables."*

CHAPTER 8
DAYS OF NOAH, DAYS OF LOT

In the gospels, Jesus gave us "signs" to look for that would let us know when the Rapture was at hand. In the gospel of Luke, Chapter 17: 26-27:

> *26 "And as it was in the days of Noe, so shall it be also in the days of the Son of man."*
>
> *27 "They did eat, they drank, they married wives, they were given in marriage, until the day that Noe entered into the ark, and the flood came, and destroyed them all."*

These verses tell us that before Noah entered the ark all of these things were occurring on the earth. The ark represents the Rapture. Before the "Tribulation" came upon the earth, God removed Noah and his family from destruction and judgment, because they were righteous people.

In Noah's day people were eating and drinking. Today it seems there are more and more restaurants and most of them are full. To get a seat in most of them you have to get on a waiting list. In Noah's day people were getting married. To me this is talking about social activity. It seems that our society has become a big party, all the time. Today, people are so caught up in "feeding" their fleshly desires that they do not even realize that Jesus is coming for his church, and that those left behind will go through a destructive tribulation period. As in Noah's day, the people did not realize destruction was coming until it was too late. Look at verse 28–30 in the same chapter:

> 28 "Likewise also as it was in the days of Lot; they did eat, they drank, they bought, they sold, they planted, they builded."

> 29 "But the same day that Lot went out of Sodom it rained fire and brimstone from heaven, and destroyed them all."

30 "Even thus shall it be in the day when the Son of man is revealed."

Again, Jesus says that when he comes for the church, the Rapture will be like the days of Noah and Lot. Did you notice that the days of Lot were similar to the days of Noah? In both cases people were not thinking about the Lord, but living to please their flesh.

The Apostle Paul talked about these kinds of people in Philippians 3:19 when he said that their God was their "belly," or their fleshly appetite, and that they minded earthly things. Paul wrote the Colossians and told them to seek things which are above, and to set their affection (mind) on things above, not on things of the earth.

Thinking back to Noah and Lot, did you notice everything the people did was for human, worldly pleasure? Again, they ate and drank, married, bought, sold, planted, and builded. They were busy, but nowhere does it say that they went to church, or worshipped God, or prayed, or gave tithes and offerings: there was no mention of spiritual things.

Let's look at the days of Lot once more to see a connection to the day in which we live.

In Genesis 19 God sends angels to get Lot and his family out of Sodom before destruction comes. This is a type of rapture. We know from the Bible and history that Sodom was a place of homosexuality. In Genesis 19:4-5 it says that the men of Sodom came to Lot's house, and demanded that the "men" (angels) be sent out so they could have sexual relations with them. In Verse 8, Lot offers his two daughters to the sodomites. I believe there are two truths we see in Lot's day:

1. Homosexuals demanding their way. V 4–5.

2. The Righteous trying to appease those involved in sexual sin. V 8.

As for Noah, he was a preacher of righteousness. (See II Peter 2:5.)

Just as in the days of Noah, today there are few people preaching righteousness, telling people to repent and live right. The days of Noah and the days of Lot are very similar to the days we are living in now. We need to get caught up in the lifestyle Jesus said in Luke 21:34–36:

> *34 "… and take heed to yourselves, lest at anytime your hearts be overcharged with surfeiting, and drunkenness, and cares of this life, and so that day come upon you unawares."*

> *35 "For as a snare shall it come on all them that dwell on the face of the whole earth."*

> *36 "Watch ye therefore, and pray always, that ye may be accounted worthy to escape all these things that shall come to pass, and to stand before the Son of man."*

Do not get caught up in the cares of this life. All of these are signs that cause us to declare a Rapture Watch.

CHAPTER 9
Discerning The Times

What does it mean to discern? Strong's Concordance says it means to judge. We as believers need to look at the signs, the "evidence," and judge what is being presented. The evidence could be considered weak if only one or two things the Bible talked about were happening, but with all the evidence the Bible gives us, we have to judge that the Rapture could happen at any moment.

In Mathew 16:3 Jesus said:

> *3 "And in the morning, it will be foul weather today: for the sky is red and lowering. O ye hypocrites, ye*

can discern the face of the sky; but can ye not discern the signs of the times?"

And in Luke 21:28:

28 "And when these things begin to come to pass, then look up, and lift up your heads; for your redemption draweth nigh."

We need to be those who can discern the signs. We cannot afford to stick our head in the sand and say things like, "I've been hearing about Jesus coming for fifty years and He hasn't come yet."

It is true He has not come yet, but never before have so many signs been revealed at one time, that Jesus told us to watch for. I believe if we rightly discern the signs that are present, we have to issue a Rapture Watch.

CHAPTER 10
Watch

In Mark 13, Jesus told us to watch:

32 "But of that day and that hour knoweth no man, no, not the angels which are in heaven, neither the Son, but the Father."

33 "Take ye heed, watch and pray: for ye know not when the time is."

34 "For the Son of man is as a man taking a far journey, who left his house, and gave authority to his servants, and to every man his work, and commanded the porter to watch."

35 "Watch ye therefore: for ye know not when the master of the house cometh, at even or at midnight, or at the cockcrowing, or in the morning."

36 "Lest coming suddenly he find you sleeping."

37 "And what I say unto you I say unto all, Watch."

We need to be about our Father's business (Luke 2:49). We need to discern the times. We need to watch.

CONCLUSION

Imagine watching television and this interruption comes on the screen:

"The Universal Rapture Service in Heaven has issued a Rapture Watch. This watch covers the whole world. This watch is in effect until Jesus comes for his Church. We now return you to your regular programming. Do not return to your regular life. Jesus is coming soon! .... SO WATCH!!!"

SALVATION

Get ready for the rapture by receiving Jesus as Lord of your life.

PRAY THIS PRAYER:

"Heavenly Father, I confess with my mouth, Jesus is my Lord.

I believe in my heart God raised him from the dead, and I receive him now.

Forgive me of my sin, fill me with your Holy Spirit, help me live for You all the days of my life.

In Jesus' Name, Amen."

Now live for Jesus. Find a church with a godly pastor who preaches the truth of God's word.

Keep growing in the things of God and remember that Jesus is coming soon; keep watching.

Front row: Logan, Landon, Graclynn, Colson, Hagan, Brennan, Back row: Tim, Easton, Lindsey, Pastor Tami, Pastor Chuck (Author),Heather, Jeremy, Irelyn,Trenton

BIOGRAPHY

Pastors Chuck and Tami Evaline were born again of the Spirit of God early in life, and in 1979 were baptized in the Holy Spirit. They were married August 2, 1980, and have two daughters. Heather is married to Jeremy Compton and they have four sons and one daughter: Trenton, Brennan, Hagan, Colson, and Irelyn. Their youngest daughter, Lindsey, is married to Tim Best and they have twin boys Logan and Landon, Easton, and a daughter, Graclynn. Both daughters are active in ministry.

After spending a short time as Associate and Youth Pastors at a Baptist church, in 1982 Pastors Chuck and Tami formed Resurrection Ministries as an evangelistic ministry. Resurrection Life Church was formed September of 1982 as an outreach of Resurrection Ministries. They are involved in radio ministry in the nation of Mauritius. They have also made numerous mission trips to Jamaica since 1994, which resulted in establishment of the Jamaica Pastors Encouragement Network (JPEN). JPEN sends encouraging letters and tapes each month to ministers around the world. In 2007 they made their first mission trip to Panama, and now travel there on a yearly basis.

Resurrection Ministries and Resurrection Life Church are blessed, and Pastors Chuck and Tami believe that the best is yet to come.

If we can help you in your walk with the Lord, please write me at:

Pastor Chuck Evaline
2804 Blackiston Mill Rd.
Clarksville, IN 47129
Email: info@resurrectionlife.org
Website: resurrectionlife.org   Ph. 812-283-5838